Flip the Flaps
Creepy-Crawlies

KINGFISHER

NEW YORK

KINGFISHER
LONDON & NEW YORK

Consultant: David Burnie

First published in hardback in 2008 by Kingfisher
This edition published in 2012 by Kingfisher

Distributed in the U.S. and Canada by Macmillan, 175 Fifth Ave., New York, NY 10010

Library of Congress Cataloging-in-Publication data has been applied for.

ISBN: 978-0-7534-6739-8

Kingfisher books are available for special promotions and premiums. For details contact:
Special Markets Department, Macmillan, 175 Fifth Ave., New York, NY 10010.

For more information, please visit www.kingfisherbooks.com

Printed in China
10 9 8 7 6 5 4 3 2 1
1TR/0911/UNTD/LFA/157MA

Contents

What are creepy-crawlies?

Creepy-crawlies are tiny animals such as insects and spiders. They have been on Earth for millions of years and live in all types of different places, from hot, wet jungles to cold, rocky mountains.

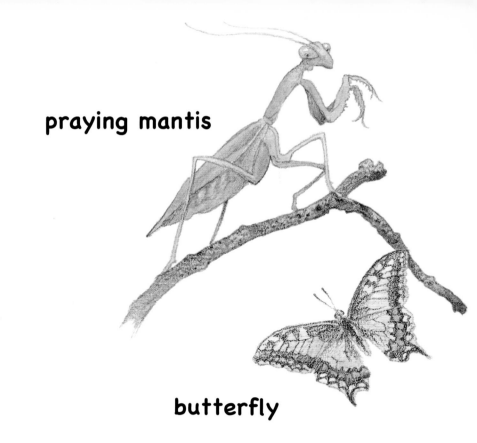

praying mantis

butterfly

two male stag beetles

4

1. How many legs
do insects have?

2. How many types
of insects are there?

3. Are beetles insects?

abdomen

head

thorax

**praying mantis
catching a butterfly**

1. All insects have six legs. They also have three parts to their bodies—a head, thorax, and abdomen.

2. There are millions of types of insects. They come in different shapes, colors, and sizes.

3. Yes. Beetles are insects. Some are very colorful; others have huge jaws.

A stag beetle attacks another with its jaws.

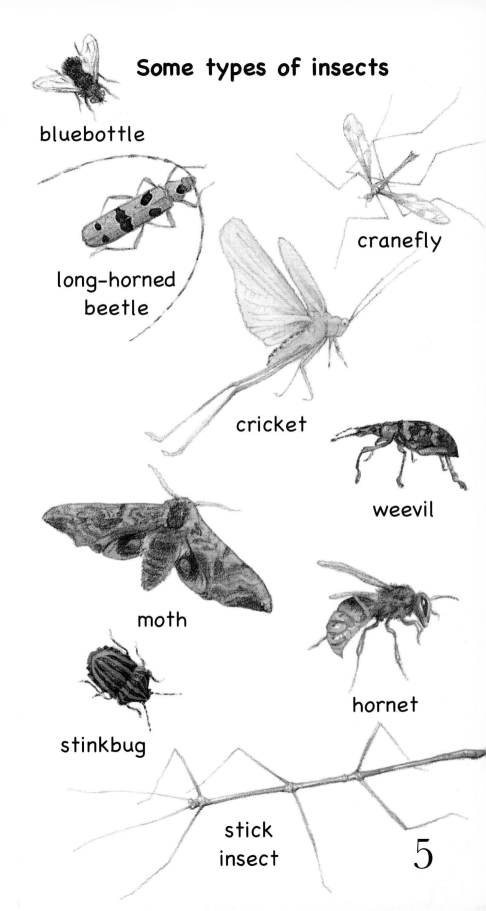

Some types of insects

bluebottle

long-horned beetle

cranefly

cricket

weevil

moth

hornet

stinkbug

stick insect

5

Ladybugs

Ladybugs are small beetles with wings. They are easy to see because they have colorful, spotted shells. Ladybugs live in gardens and meadows and have tiny mouths and a pair of jaws.

ladybug on a leaf

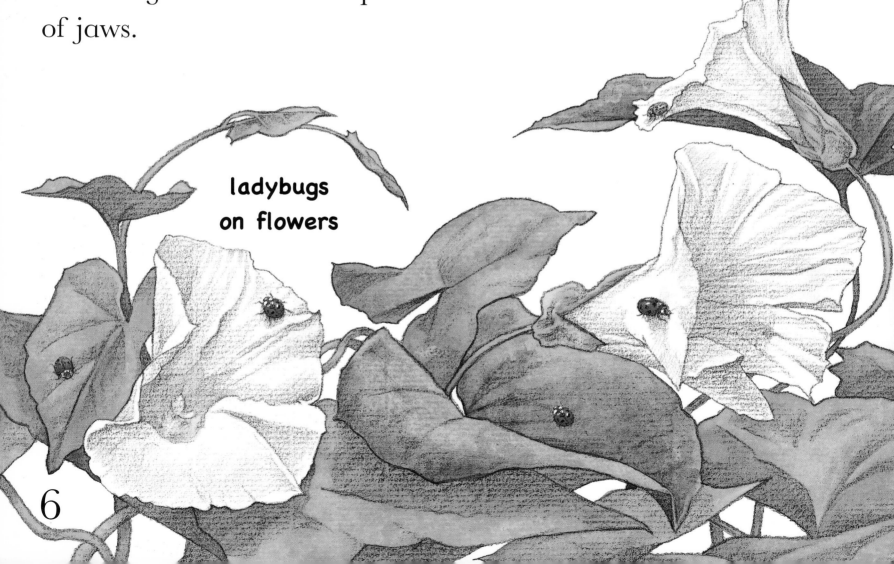

ladybugs on flowers

6

1. How do ladybugs smell, taste, and feel?

2. Can a ladybug fly?

3. What does a ladybug eat?

2. Yes. A ladybug's spotted shell is actually a hard pair of wings. They protect the softer wings underneath.

3. Ladybugs eat tiny pests that live on plants. This helps keep the plants healthy and strong.

A hungry ladybug

ladybug eating pests

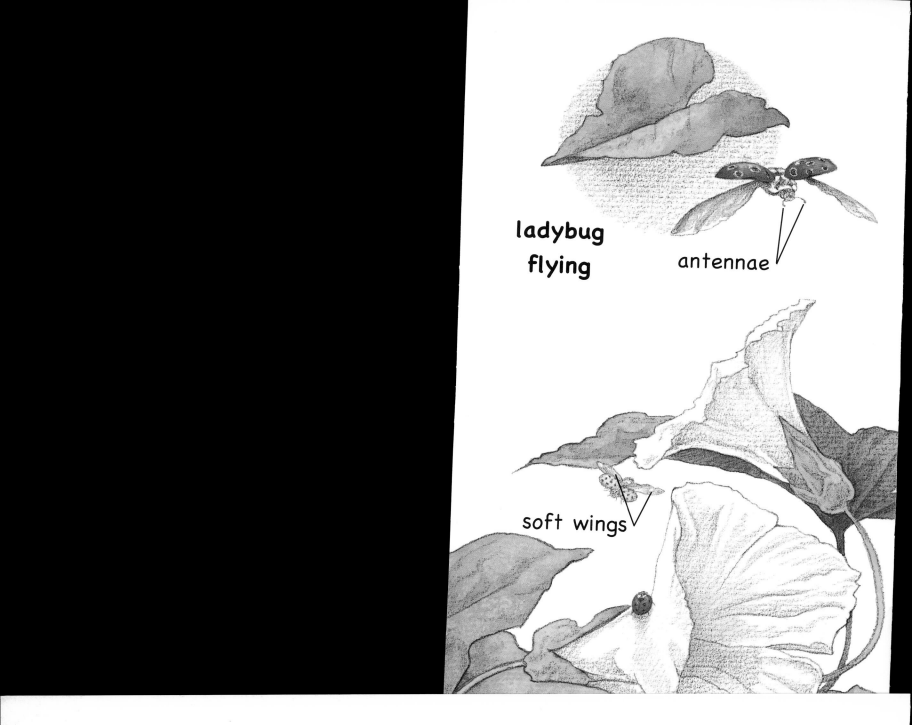

ladybug flying

antennae

soft wings

Ants

Ants are busy insects that live in large groups. Some make their nests under stones, in the ground, or inside logs or trees. Carpenter ants, or wood ants, make their nests inside a giant pile of dead leaves.

queen ant flying

carpenter ants' nest

1. Can any ants fly?

2. How many ants live in a nest?

3. Why do some ants cut up leaves?

queen ant losing
her wings

tunnels in
a carpenter
ants' nest

1. Yes. Queen ants fly away to start new nests. They lose their wings when they land.

2. Millions of ants can live in one nest. Most of these are worker ants. They take care of the queen.

3. Leafcutter ants cut up leaves with their strong jaws. Inside the nest, they use the leaves to make food.

Leafcutter ants

9

Butterflies

There are many types of butterflies. Some of them fly a long way to spend the winter in warm sunshine. Most butterflies feed on flowers. They suck up their food through their long, hollow mouth.

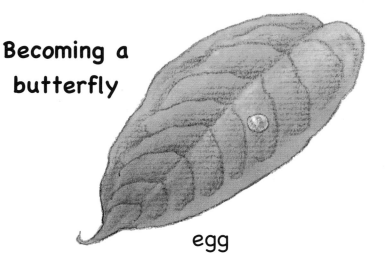

egg

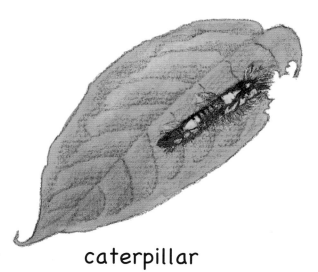

caterpillar

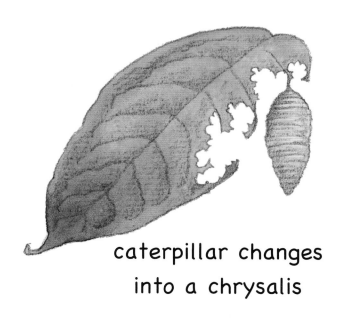

caterpillar changes into a chrysalis

butterfly on a flower

mouth curled up

10

1. How many eggs
   do butterflies lay?

2. How does a caterpillar
   turn into a butterfly?

3. Which butterfly has
   extrastrong wings?

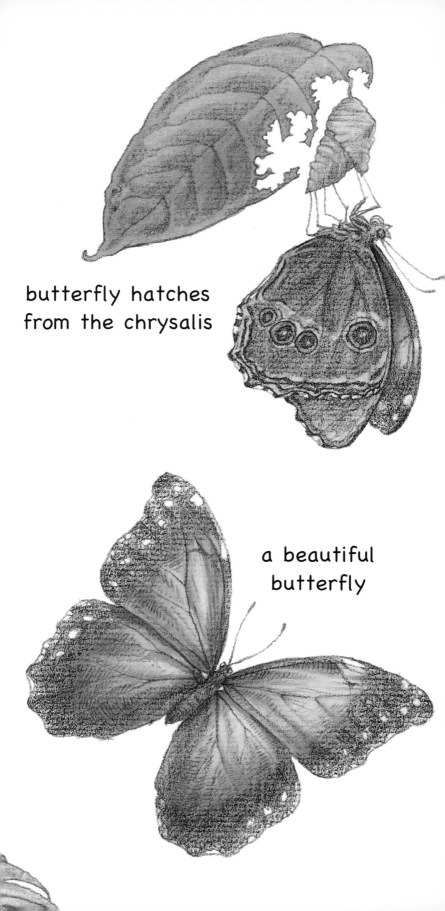

butterfly hatches
from the chrysalis

a beautiful
butterfly

1. Some butterflies lay one egg at a time. Others can lay hundreds of eggs on one leaf!

2. A caterpillar changes into a chrysalis, which then turns into a butterfly.

3. A monarch butterfly has strong wings. Each winter it flies thousands of miles.

Monarch butterflies flying south in the winter

11

Spiders

There are more than 40,000 different types of spiders. They can be smaller than the tip of a pencil or bigger than a dinner plate. All spiders can grow a new leg if one breaks.

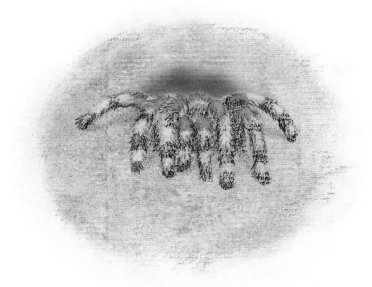

Mexican redknee tarantula

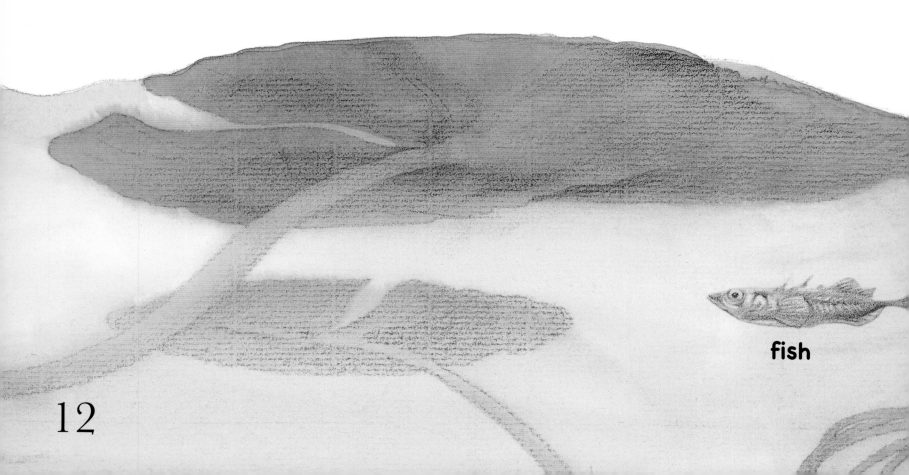

fish

12

1. Do all spiders live on webs?

2. How does a spider build a web?

3. Why do water spiders have long, hairy legs?

water spider
in its air
bubble nest

Mexican redknee tarantula
about to grab a cricket

water spider
catching a fish

1. No. Many spiders, such as this Mexican redknee tarantula, live in burrows underground.

2. A spider makes a line of silk inside its body. It sticks the silk from one place to another to build a web.

3. A water spider's long, hairy legs help the spider catch its food.

Building a web

building lines of silk

the web is finished

Honeybees

Honeybees make their
nests out of wax. Inside
the nest, there are thousands
of small spaces, called cells.
Some cells are used to store
honey, and the queen bee
lays her eggs in other cells.

honeybee nest

honeybees flying

14

1. How do honeybees
talk to each other?

2. How do honeybees
make honey?

3. What keeps a queen
bee busy in the spring?

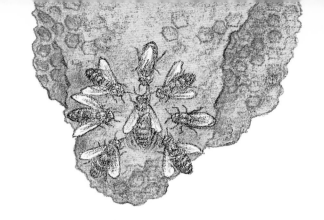

honeybee dancing

**honeybee
sucking nectar**

1. Honeybees do a special dance to tell other bees in the nest where the best flowers are growing.

2. Honeybees suck nectar, a sugary water, from flowers. They turn this nectar into honey inside their bodies.

3. In the spring, a queen bee can lay more than two thousand eggs a day.

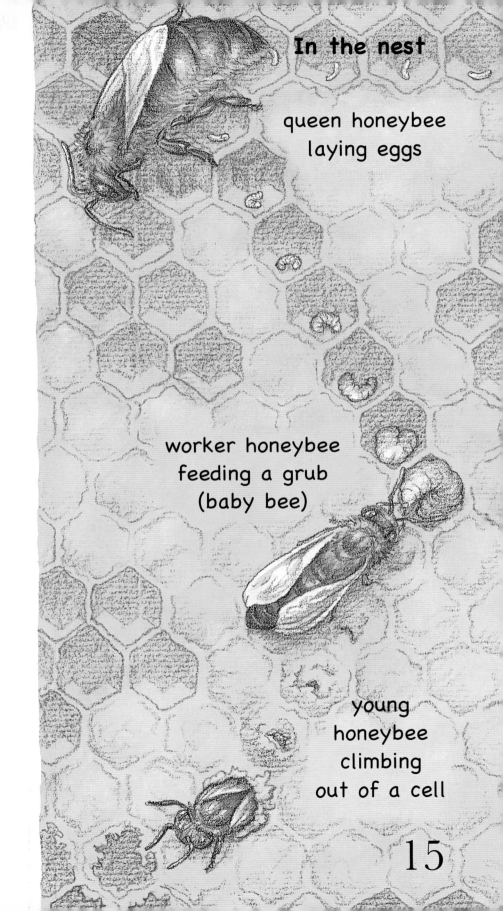

In the nest

queen honeybee laying eggs

worker honeybee feeding a grub (baby bee)

young honeybee climbing out of a cell

15

Dragonflies

Dragonflies live close to ponds and lakes. They are speedy hunters that feed on smaller insects. Some hover in the air and chase their food. Others lie in wait, snatching up insects that come too close.

dragonfly

Once dragonflies were huge.

16

1. Do dragonflies have eyes?

2. Why do dragonflies have four wings?

3. How long have dragonflies lived on Earth?

eye

dragonfly

Dragonflies are smaller today.

1. Dragonflies have the largest eyes of all insects.

2. Dragonflies can move their wings in different directions. They can fly forward or backward to escape danger.

3. Dragonflies have lived on Earth for 300 million years. They were even around before the dinosaurs!

A dragonfly in danger

hungry toad lying in wait

dragonfly flying backward

Index